we are all things and all people
by mackenzie kristjon

we are all things and all people
By Mackenzie Kristjon.

ISBN 978-09689-119-3-8

Cover image by Juliana Lachance.

COASTLINE PUBLISHING
www.coastline-publishing.com | www.thismaddesire.net
for a good time, give us a call. operators are standing by...

we are all things and all people

Dear reader,

The following is a series of poetic-assemblages that I have composed through the years. Because I predominantly think of myself as a songwriter, most of my writing is fodder for lyrics. Nevertheless, these pieces seemed to have taken on their own life as poems.

The first poem "the words fluttered..." was originally published in an anthology of Guelph-area authors entitled *Words and Wonders* back in the olden-timey days of 2001. At the time, I was living in the hamlet of Eden Mills (or "Eden Thrills" as I used to call it) near Guelph, Ontario.

Here and there over the years, I've dusted off some of these poems and had a few people review them. In particular, Christine Pountney and Tom Shea had some good suggestions. Christine was the Author-in-Residence at the Hamilton Public Library at one point and was very insightful. Tom is a local English teacher in Hamilton who I know from our local music scene.

More recently, I've retitled the collection. Originally it was called "burn your neighbours. read their books." Nonetheless I've since felt that "we are all things and all people" captures more the way I naturally feel about the world.

Life is too short. Enjoy it!

-Mackenzie Kristjon, 2018

the words fluttered and sang to me all morning

1. we are all things and all people

it was as easy as they said it would be. i closed my eyes and felt myself slide in all directions of space and time. one second i was in paris at a café drinking the night with my skin; simultaneously i was adrift on a raft to the west of japan, exploring the pacific with my elongated toes, tickling fish, rubbing tentacles with initiated octopi.

for my next experiment, i brought with me my possessions. my books soaked into the sea and their sentences floated to the surface free of syntax and stability. in this new watery text i felt myself merge with the author, her tongue slithering like sex through my soul. i opened my mouth to cry and felt stars sink into my panic and tranquility. we combed the ocean floor for clues as to how to fish the poetry from our books. this took one thoughtless glance and up we were adrift on clouds, marveling at the new wings we could sleep on.

spreading into the world was as easy as (everything is all right everything is) closing my eyes.

2. we are all one

i was an only child in my head and so i invented playthings —machines of my psyche. outsourcing my self, multiplying my personalities, i became more self-sufficient, better able to sustain my growth into the next fis(i)cal year.

3. except for her

my love moves through the window, graceless and old, pondering the pavement, spreading her arms (now graceful and bold) she catches flying cats and purrs like the whirring of electricities and imaginations.

the time for wanting is upon us.

love is a ghost slowly solidifying

love is a ghost slowly solidifying, being born again. it lived before, it was murdered, it waits in the shadows to be (re)discovered.. it beckons with silence, with patience.. will it be seen? (wondering and hoping and wishing) love is a prayer behind my lips that i recite when your legs beguile my wits.. in praise of a violent god that shakes me, makes me shiver as it finds resurrection in the slow, soft connection of our aching (dripping down your) bodies entwined by love, lassoed by some outlaw love, held at gunpoint by an impatient now love that wills to wish again.

love is a wish that swims through rivers. its eyes are fish and it feels the violent kicks, the sinking nothing. cocktail dramas erupt and don't you know that love wants up? it wants to possess, to be possessed, to be the only thing that could come between us.

"popcorn nostalgia"

the stars were going mad, all swirly-eyed and popcorn for brains,
butter dripping from their ears. and three cheers for the director
who conquered the armoured egos of a thousand (self) righteous
artistes.. the slow dim realization that they were pawns made
them ever so jealous, darling. ever–so–jealous..

it wasn't long before one of them decided to form a un-
ion, art by democracy! all of the director's ideas had to be credited
to the union. fine…

except that the director was sleeping with the producer
and the producer wanted nothing but the best for her director..
but you know how directors are.. i mean, really darling, all out for
the glory of appearing on entertainment tonight or in entertain-
ment weekly. they're no better than the actors.. ain't none of these
movie types appearing in art weekly darling. not a one! the actors
thought they were revolutionary but they just hadn't caught up
with their own fictions yet.

thinking of a good way to say "hello"

i've been thinking about ways to make sunshine into solid gold
that could be switched back and forth between gold currency and

light depending on which would be more illuminating,

riches or vision.

the dream city

(and i'm very sick of the word "truth")

the malaise is the primary reason why the citizenry opted to make their city mobile.. to keep the evil twin of shadowy reproduction at bay, to leave no xerox trace, to be self-sufficient, to not have the moral plague of shadow to steal its glory.

and so, in this dream city, there is no night. caught under the sun all day, the citizens never sleep.. always they must be working to move everything around. purity is difficult to maintain. the constant cleaning, the constant moving of buildings one inch to the west, one inch to the west.. uprooting parks and rivers.. even those who were trained in the arts and non-labouring professions have been made to give up their vocations —not without some highly understandable embitterment.. the cost of freedom is an enormous undertaking. in fact, the only thing that keeps the tension bearable is the unimaginable promise that the next move will be the final one.

the divine city

through wild cities race the children of god. they will overtake
the cities, make them slither back.. the snake cities –the charm-
ing children.. the buildings will rise (some say "loom") and dance
(some say "quake") and women will fall (some say "leap") from
the building-tops only to snap their necks on the silent streets..
the men all cry out in unison: "why must so many immaculate
conceptions create such travesty?"

the trouble is that each of these women felt unfathom-
ably deceived. if honesty were not so lacking in the sinister and
corrupt cities and times into which they had been born, they may
have been more forgiving of the fact that their immaculate child
of god was not the second coming but one of many such second
comings. jesus christ was so ..so singular unlike these multiple
messiahs.. divine repetition (some even thought "indifference")..
one can easily understand how this would diminish (some would
say "devastate") the pride and self-worth of these women who had
imagined themselves to be the mothers of a new god–an utter fic-
tion, a complete fraud.

"why did he do this?" the men wondered as they picked
up their women. the children continued to laugh and dance with
delight. the city would soon be theirs to rule.. in time, the men
would become completely entranced by these children, swooning
at their every word, servile to the end..

the technicians were baffled when they stepped into the room. "everything is suspiciously the same!" they exclaimed. "almost as if someone had pulled everything apart and put it back together in exactly the same way as it was, not a molecule out of place!"

and it was true that this is exactly what had happened, for in truth, someone had come along and disrupted the contents of this room. the curiosity had been overwhelming. oh the lovely secret machinery that softly purred in this technical house, a house described by the villagers as "pure technique". oh the wonder to see the inner workings of it all (and to tell the others!). the joy to share in the secret knowledge!

one could certainly empathize.

the trespassers to knowledge had indeed snuck inside to exorcise the mystery that had haunted them–the spirit which guided them here. diligently they worked, pulling the tops off of everything. no part was left unturned.

however, something had gone horribly wrong. every piece that was removed revealed the outdoors. there was nothing under anything! "this must be a trick!" one of the trespassers cried out. "how can there be nothing here? nothing under the surface of anything but that which was already there supposed?"

with this deep humiliation behind them, they slowly put every piece back in place, careful to leave no trace. when they returned to the village, the villagers whispered to them "what did you see?" and "what was there?" some of the trespassers were silent on the subject, some said that the truth could not be explained but only experienced, but one declared that the technicians' home was evil, that it was impossible, and that it should be burned.

and so the villagers held a meeting. in the end all the trespassers concurred that this house should be burned. without further ado, torches were lit and the villagers paraded to the technicians' house, setting it ablaze.

but the house never burned. the technicians hid in the

trees where they would not be found and waited for the villagers to lose interest, which eventually they did. deflated, the villagers trudged back home. when they awoke the next morning, the sun shone through their windows, birds sang in the trees, and the air carried the scent of fresh-cut flowers. the bitterness of the previous night had been displaced by a quiet acceptance and rejuvenation of spirit, a new sense of wonder..

none of the villagers could remember anything about that house and when they walked by it, they could not see it, and so it was never mentioned again..

grasshoppers and k-mart shoppers

grasshoppers and k-mart shoppers, i have an announcement to make. the story will be closing soon. please take your purchases to the check-out aisle where the ducks will wring you through. please sign your cheques with blood. no shoplifiting–strictly forbidden. there are alligators at the door trained to snap at the sound of the alarm. they are live animals; treat them with utmost respect. go back to your communities, drink your gin–tell your neighbours and friends: this story will come to an end.

with or without them. if there is a special someone who doesn't know their place in your heart, now would be the time to stretch your hearts and conversations to include them. did you forget your gifts in your rush?

thank everyone you appreciate. move up the corporate ladder at the speed of light. break the fourth wall. interact. tell others your dreams. work together. feed an animal.

we value your business so please come back tomorrow. this is a recording.

i haven't yet told you about my dreams

there were these poor little boys all dressed up in kilts and they were holding flowers and bemoaning the "system" which was conspiring against them. it was telling them that flowers were for girls and that religion was for optimists but the wild-eyed youths, pessimistic by nature, did not like to be excluded from anything, even the sacraments, and so they put flowers in the hair of all the singing choir girls and drank the blood of christ gaily for the remainder of the day until the voices of the beautiful choir girls began to crack from singing so loudly at the top of their lungs about how much they loved love.

god kept smiling down but talking up a storm until eventually his words drenched the drunken boys who all decided to be-come prophets and tell people about their visions of ecstasy and traveling and sangria.

(they try so hard

but they still know it's actually begun)

rimbaud and a bottle of wine

developing a taste for enormity, they sailed great big clipper ships down streams of wreckage, overturning small joys wherever they went, laughing, laughing. enlarging the stream into a putrid river of filth, ever deeper, channelling far into the countryside, devastating small farms owned by even tinier (some might say "miniature") farmers. string them up! what good are they? the bigger, the better, the murkier, the more obtuse the more. the painfully more.

aboard this ship as a wayward passenger i learned to invent light. in our wake we would leave villages burned and spoiled, covered in garbage. with a glance, i would rebuild the homes and restore faith in miracles.

the pious who had stumblingly devolved into drunkards i would wash in smiles of dancing purity. their eyes smiled back at me, displaying new colours.

my captain wore noise for a jacket. it was years before it gave him peace. it was then that i retired from my tireless career as a miracle worker.

the city of burning love

they pause at the city gates. the moment will burn in their memories forever–the night they discarded not a garment but replaced one skin with another. the shouting from field to field and the emergent realization that it couldn't happen too soon. so sick were the unimpassioned lovers, lost in the routine, weary with repetition, their once unbroken gazes gone slack with disappointment, listless and wandering. where the burning fire of love goes unfed, the burning fire of kerosene seems its most worthy replacement.

and so, to rekindle their passions, the lovers burned the city down -a volcanic inferno of exploding glass and quietly smouldering houses. goodbye to old flames, they said..

out of the ashes would come new loves, new memories, new ways to dream.. (now the lovers meet in secret and though they say nothing, the new geographies of their bodies invite much to be explored..)

difference is an evil to be overcome

i can remember the evil bickering over nothing, the flash changes
in personality (to-day i'm a queen! to-morrow a jack!) i waited
until my eyes fell out and my hair fell out and my brains leaked
out and my heart dribbled out of my mouth and my fingers fell
off and now we are all the same so sickeningly the same so much
the same no one can differentiate anymore no divisions no sun no
sand no way to make it reappear here in the sea of similitude and
no words no bickering all vacant now all out of opinions now just
beliefs we all hold true because there can be no opinions if there
is no opposition no difference anyway
some of this text also appears in Kings & Queens -i was using cut-up
machines to make some of these...

21

Kings & Queens

Oh how the seeds of dysfunction cause the trees to twist and
my hair falls out and my brain leaks out and my eyes close and
all the water tears out and my flesh falls off and my bones crack
and soon I am dust scattered to the wind. When my soul leans
forward, it feels like it is looking at a powerful mirror that im-
proves its image. Again it starts. A little mumbled comment while
walking up the stairs—the lonesome, "I was just asking you a
favour but you are probably too busy lurking in the shadows,
humming not singing a short, repetitive phrase. A short, repeti-
tive phrase and how it longs for a woman to caress it, to make it
feel loved again, to make it feel whole, to make it sing again, to
take me there. Insight and power; it used to take me here. Now it
is like being skinned alive. It used to feel triumphant. And now?"
But my soul hurts, quietly cowers take me down all broken in a
corner wishing everything were alleyways.

Make it tremble with anticipation as it swallows pain and spits
joy. How it longs for a gentle, 'I've always loved you. I loved you
before we ever met. I loved you when I was five years old' and I
hope that sweetness is about what happens when dread and con-
tagion fade. Brains have leaked out anyway. *Put like a tumbling
flower through that dress.*

Leave your old body behind. Pick love and embrace the kissing
miracle. Bodies ("i've got you under my—") deep in the heart of
(take me) where its bones still soul still claims ownership of its
skin.

Readers Anonymous

Reading is always an act of destruction. Only through reading can you feel the immensity and scope of full lives being lived with blood and bones.

Fiction pulls you into an entire safe world of someone else's dreams and possibilities. The possibilities are what of course generate the allure, the impact, the anticipation.

But it isn't real (!) and that's a shame. People should spend more time living. The dramas can be just as sophisticated and can be equally compelling so long as you yourself are willing to imbue moments with self-serving meaning. So long as when her eyes dart from you when you turn to her that it means something. So long as a dream of buying lipstick is a revelation of the highest order. So long as when you see her she smiles and really it's a car crash.

Otherwise, life is not that entertaining.

It's easier, perhaps more realistic—but remember, fiction is just supposed to be plausible—to think that she was looking at something else, just had a weird dream, and smiles at everyone in the same way always. It's also less controversial and then..

Get me a drink and a novel. I'm jumping through that window again.

Reality is shocking

Reality is a shocking thing to take. And love?

Even worse. Who would ever wish it on anyone? It's all heartbreak and chaos until it ends. Who could live like that? Worse –who would ever bring children into such a scenario? The best parents are never in love. They are always "parents", not "people". And they are never in love. They have a job to do and they do it well. All that nurturing and caring and who has time for anything else? Time for especially love. Impossible!

My love waltzes through dark dancehalls and swims in dark rivers and thinks dark thoughts and drinks dark drinks and dreams dark dreams. My love, mother, artist, wife.

In my secret dreams

In my secret dreams, you walk through the door as though you live here. Armed with good intentions and love, you disarm me. Your smile arrests me.
Even when you are not with me, this happens. Every night.

In your secret captivity, I twist and turn and watch my life fall apart. My line of credit disappears, my hair recedes, my heart stops.
Especially when you are here with me, this happens. Every day.

Love fails, intelligence fails, insults fail, threats fail, anger fails. Everything fails to stop it. It repeats with mechanical precision. History crushes us both.
Even when you are not here with me, this happens. In every way with every fight.

I opened my heart to a bird song. Its breath was even beautiful, but all birds can panic and songs can turn to shrieks and the fragile flutter of wings can be lethal when let loose inside. Outside, it may flee, may find direction, may find calm, may sing again.
But I still wait to see you crash through my window as though you can forgive fear.

!the love bank, the love government, the love laws, the love institutions, the love doctors, the love saxophones, the love melodies, the love potions, the love cafeterias, the love revolutions, the love new york, the love and holy eternity, the love breath on my neck, the love visionaries, the love abyss, the love forgiveness, the love supernatural suffering and kindness.

Waiting for you

Lanterns shine in my window when you walk through the forest.
I don't always know that you are coming.
It's my quiet contribution to hope.

Stop.watch

The procession of this evil in my heart
Ticks like a time bomb & then I will start
To quiver & quibble, to drip & to dribble.
My tongue lashes forward, let loose like a riddle.
Nothing can stop me now. I'm starting to listen
To this voice in my heart that tells me to quicken
This procession of faith,
This parade of conformity,
This panic of hate, this betrayal of normalcy.

The ticktock clicking of teeth in my ears.
The tangled to terrible force of my years.
It's hard to believe that this will not come true.
That my heart will lie broken, jealous of you.
That my eyes will not open, jealous of you.

Where do we go from here?

I ask you to leave as I find you alarming
And what I caan't believe is quite just how charming
Can ever you be, you arrest and disarm me
Oh I can't let you go you now my oh my darling!

Never asked I of you to please police me
But never asked I of you to then release me
Into the world in sudden increasing
Increments of love that gather unceasing.

sex birds

time wears a sly disguise..

an invisible cloak that only becomes revealed in old photographs..
how did I not catch it? (and the scars on my back reveal little)
she didn't mean to I didn't mean to time didn't mean anything
anymore anyway slipinto thefinalsolutiontheultimate timetrap

(birds sing as though every moment they might forget their tune
become tuneless become aged stay in tune keep in tune give them
room

vroom vroom vrooomm (va va)… ul uh

science is a learning curve for the soul

the time between two kisses is a measure of
"oh honey you make me feel divine".
the inverse of t α Love.

30

the momentum of each kiss is a measure of
"oh.. mmmmm.."
p α Lust.

the relative humidity of each kiss is a measure of
(please you're boring me).
1/RH α (p y b m).

love vs. sports

tell me
(and this is true of course)
tell me
love is better than sports.

weakness and excuses

it's not my fault.
oh I'm just angry because
it's true. I AM being
weak. I am making
wrong and wasteful
decisions. stop
pointing them out. stop it, stop it, stop it!

(you see my neurons are disappearing, eaten up by aging, by
mind-sucking parasites, by aliens who use me as a test subject, by
insects who burrow into my head replacing the space in my brain
with their corpses –"I can't breathe in here!" I often hear them
complain inside my head just before they convulse, quiver, and
then silently go..)

buttercats

when love becomes a parachute
it falls flat

when love is a butterfly
it feeds the love-starved cat.

new language of math

when all the boys tell her that
(they love her),
she just blushes and giggles because
she believes it not to be true. she thinks it
a cute way to say "hello". like
it's a new language of math in which numbers
were replaced
by line-ups of desperately eligible bachelors.

are they too ritzy for you?

are they too
ritzy for you?
we can't all be filthy rich you know
we can't all own flashy sports
cars and islands in the south
pacific and bathe in marble
Jacuzzis zipping (rum and scotch) by
personal lear jets
can't complain
no
can't comp(or try to explain
the weathertimemoney)slain
in the battlefields of glitz

don't say that

don't say that
      -I'm not
you're beautiful
     -this is true
I really mean it
      -I know you do
I'd like to frame you
      -please
and hang you in a gallery..
       -stop you're embarrassing me
and show you to everyone!
      -stop.
did I say something wrong?
       -no. well…
if I'm excited it's because I love you and I think you're beautiful.
       -don't say that
but I am.

springtime television set

you need to turn me
                         on
and I need to be smacked
if I am not turning
on when you turn me
on (my wiring must
be confused because you
should be able to turn me
on?)

separation number two

we are
autonomous
countries but our
kisses pushed the
boundaries and established a free trade
zone. at first you complained that I
was not global enough in my thinking
for you but soon we were exchanging political
secrets and our
borders became UN
guarded.
our intentions began to over
lap and our maplines
blurred. this was not
always easy, given our exceeding complexity and torrid
history

"I love you"
-moi aussi

-je t'adore
"don't leave me"

burn your neighbours. read their books.

1. open their eyes. covet a little.

they turned the lights off on the sinister streets in hopes that
they might vanish. while the whore culture thrived anyway and
backstabbed the suburbs -fucking their husbands and enchanting
the young with their gypsy mouths and leopard skin drugs, the
women of god took a magic carpet ride to cyberspace. there they
established a virtual haven from the seductive torment that throbs
in the dark behind the curtain of disaster. as they felt trapped by
their bodiless existence, they soon realized that life was too long
to suffer like this.

2. learn your neighbours. breed their books.

the shocking relief of spreading oneself too thin makes it impossi-
ble to think that another could merely begin. beginning -mere be-
ginning!- seemed such a road paved with sorrow that they sought
to entrance the hopeful onto their new path of bodily pleasure,
physical lust, sinful salvation.

3. turn off the lights. feel the world.

the last resort

the last resort is prime
(just over past the)
real estate the best
on the beach
(undersand?)
not every customer can always
afford it but when
the need arises

they always find a way to vacation here

About the author

Mackenzie Kristjon is a songwriter that performs under the rock and roll brand This Mad Desire (www.thismaddesire.net). He has performed in Canada, the USA, and various European countries.

He has published *The Culinary Saga of New Iceland: Recipes from the Shores of Lake Winnipeg* by Kristin Olafson-Jenkyns and *Falcons Gold: Canada's First Olympic Hockey Heroes* by Kathleen Arnason. He also put together *The Ultimate Icelandic-North American Directory*.

Mac grew up in Manitoba and feels a strong connection to his Icelandic-Canadian roots. He currently resides in Hamilton, Ontario.

Life is too short. Enjoy it.

www.ingramcontent.com/pod-product-compliance
Lightning Source LLC
Chambersburg PA
CBHW051741040426
42447CB00008B/1240